Why Are There Stars and Stripes on the American Flag?

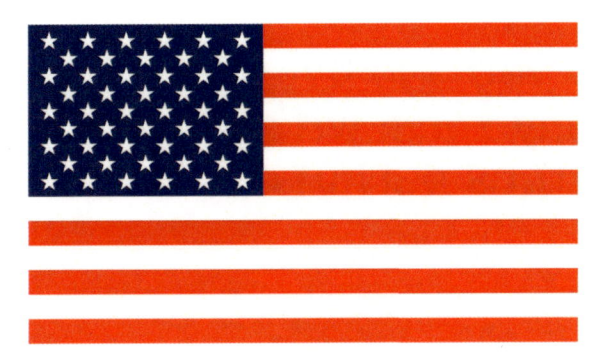

by R. Kaye Springer

Why Are There Stars and Stripes? by R Kaye Springer

www.RKayeSpringer.com

© 2020 R Kaye Springer

All rights reserved. No portion of this book may be reproduced in any form without permission from the publisher, except as permitted by U.S. copyright law.

ISBN: 978-1-64945-028-9

Why Are There Stars and Stripes on the American Flag?

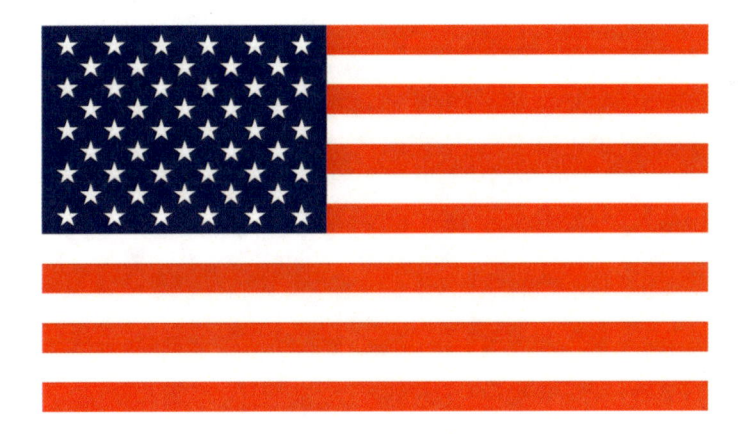

by R. Kaye Springer

The 50 stars

in that
dark blue square

Shine for

every state that's there!

The Thirteen Stripes

7 red,
white 6

Stand for
thirteen colonies

That started
our country
in

1776.

Now, RED
and
WHITE
and
BLUE

Stand for **BRAVE** and KIND and TRUE.

And every time you show you are

you put the shine in every star!

Thank You!

These Are The Original

13 Colonies

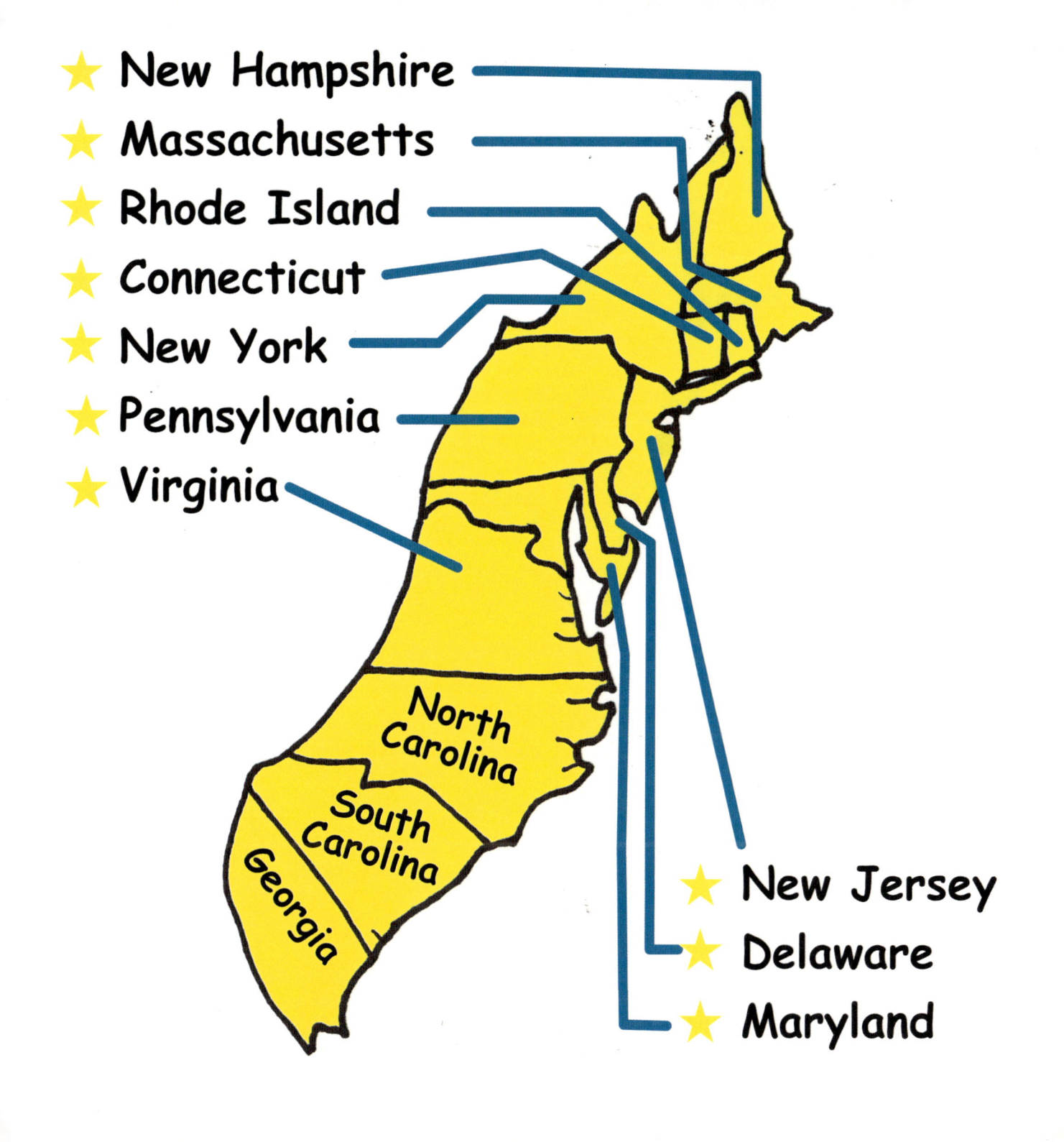

★ New Hampshire
★ Massachusetts
★ Rhode Island
★ Connecticut
★ New York
★ Pennsylvania
★ Virginia

North Carolina
South Carolina
Georgia

★ New Jersey
★ Delaware
★ Maryland

These are now the names of our fifty states:
- ★ Alabama
- ★ Alaska
- ★ Arizona
- ★ Arkansas
- ★ California

★ Colorado
★ Connecticut
★ Delaware
★ Florida
★ Georgia
★ Hawaii
★ Idaho
★ Illinois

★ Indiana
★ Iowa
★ Kansas
★ Kentucky
★ Louisiana
★ Maine
★ Maryland
★ Massachusetts

★ Michigan
★ Minnesota
★ Mississippi
★ Missouri
★ Montana
★ Nebraska
★ Nevada
★ New Hampshire

★ New Jersey
★ New Mexico
★ New York
★ North Carolina
★ North Dakota
★ Ohio
★ Oklahoma
★ Oregon

★ Pennsylvania
★ Rhode Island
★ South Carolina
★ South Dakota
★ Tennessee
★ Texas
★ Utah
★ Vermont

★ Virginia
★ Washington
★ West Virginia
★ Wisconsin
★ Wyoming

Now name
the state
you
live in:

_____

If you liked the verses,
cartoons, and
character building
in this book
look for other titles
from R. Kaye Springer,
such as

Where's My Other Sock?

A fun look at perseverance with cartoons and verse

and...

Hoggy Doggy Meets The Mooch Pooch

A fun look at friendship with cartoons and verse

Made in the USA
Coppell, TX
14 October 2021